Joan Denise Moriarty
Ireland's First Lady of Dance

Edited by Ruth Fleischmann

with contributions by
Séamas de Barra,
Patricia Crosbie, Ruth Fleischmann,
Monica Gavin, David Wallace
& Digital photography by Max Fleischmann

**LIBRARIES
LEABHARLANNA**

Cork City Council | Comhairle Cathrach Chorcaí

2012

JOAN DENISE
MORIARTY

CENTENARY 2012

Published 2012 by
Cork City Libraries / Leabharlanna Cathrach Chorcaí
57-61 Grand Parade,
Cork

www.corkcitylibraries.ie

ISBN 978-0-9549847-8-6

Digital photography: Max Fleischmann
Design: edit+ www.stuartcoughlan.com
Printed in Ireland by City Print Ltd, Cork

LIBRARIES
LEABHARLANNA

CORK CITY COUNCIL | COMHAIRLE CATHRACH CHORCAÍ

CORK MUSIC ARCHIVE
CARTLANN CHEOIL CHORCAÍ

Contents

Foreword

Cork City Council is pleased to support the celebrations marking the centenary of Joan Denise Moriarty's birth and as Lord Mayor I am honoured to pen this foreword to a remarkable woman.

For fifty years she worked to make our city a centre of dance, opening up new worlds to young people from all walks of life. Her enthusiasm and generosity of spirit were as strong at the end of her wonderful career as they had been at the start. She brought rich and colourful entertainment to the audiences at the annual Cork Ballet Week in the Opera House, accompanied by the Cork Symphony Orchestra. From there they brought their shows to many Munster towns. From 1959-1964 and 1974-1989 her two professional ballet companies brought dance from Cork to the whole of Ireland and into schools across the country.

She had a dual dance heritage, being not only a ballet dancer, but also a champion Irish step-dancer as well as a traditional musician: a prize-winning solo war pipes player. She brought traditional Irish dance and music not only to Irish television and to our Cork International Choral Festival, but also to French and German folk dance festivals in the 1950s and 1960s.

She collaborated with the Cork musicians Seán Ó Riada, Bernard Geary and Aloys Fleischmann, with that great writer and actor Micheál MacLiammóir, who did our city the honour of claiming to have been born here, and the artists from our Crawford School of Art Marshall and Clare Hutson, Frank Sanquest and Patrick Murray.

She was the choreographer of 115 ballets. Her *Playboy of the Western World*, with The Chieftains, was seen here in Cork, in Dublin, in Belfast, in New York, in London and in Rennes. In 1979 she was awarded an honorary doctorate for her service to the arts by the National University of Ireland.

One of the centres of the commemorations is the Firkin Crane, a historic building refurbished, due to her vision, as a centre of dance. Cork City Ballet, directed by her student Alan Foley, is organising two major gala performances with distinguished guest artists, and many others events, demonstrating how vibrant Moriarty's legacy in the city is.

Cork City Libraries is the other centre of the Moriarty celebrations. The Central Library now houses the Moriarty Papers, the largest historical ballet collection in the country. This significant legacy is being archived and digitised and will be made available on the Libraries' Moriarty website as part of the city's rich cultural heritage, thus creating a lasting memorial to the woman who gave a lifetime of selfless service to her art, her city and her country. I thank all those who have helped to honour Joan Denise Moriarty and to ensure that her memory will continue to be cherished in our city and beyond.

Cllr Terry Shannon, *Lord Mayor of Cork*

The conferring of honorary doctorates by the National University of Ireland in Dublin on 5 April 1979 to (l to r) Anthony Lucas, director of the National Museum of Ireland, Joan Denise Moriarty, artistic director of the Irish Ballet Company; on the right, T.K. Whitaker, chancellor of the National University of Ireland

Introduction

Cork City Libraries are delighted to publish *Joan Denise Moriarty: Ireland's First Lady of Dance* to mark the centenary of her birth. Joan Denise Moriarty was, as Ruth Fleischmann writes in this book "the central figure of ballet in Ireland for a quarter of a century". She was a dancer, piper, teacher and founder and director of this country's first professional ballet company.

In 2010 Cork City Libraries published *The Fleischmanns, A Remarkable Cork Family*, to mark the centenary of the birth of Aloys Fleischmann Jnr. We publish this book as a companion to that earlier publication, conscious of the many parallels between these two artists, creators, and indomitable activists for an Ireland that would have music, dance and the arts at the heart of daily life.

This book brings together five major pieces on Joan Denise Moriarty, and five shorter pieces, beginning with a tribute by Domy Reiter-Soffer, collaborator and friend from 1962 to 1989. These contributions tell of her life, the companies she founded and led, the music, and the dance. The book concludes with four short pieces on her legacy, still vibrant in the twenty-first century.

The Joan Denise Moriarty Collection was donated to Cork City Libraries in 2010; we are currently sorting and listing this invaluable collection of letters, programmes, photographs, choreography and scores, and will begin the digitization of the material in 2012 as a major contribution to the centenary year. The material will then be permanently available to researchers and other interested persons through our website www.corkcitylibraries.ie. Cork City Libraries will also mount a major exhibition on Dr Moriarty's life and work during 2012, bringing her story to a new generation.

Liam Ronayne
Cork City Librarian

www.corkcitylibraries.ie
www.aloysfleischmann.ie

A Tribute to Joan Denise Moriarty

Domy Reiter-Soffer

Joan Denise Moriarty – dancer, musician, teacher, choreographer and director – was one of the most important figures in promoting the art of dance in Ireland. I collaborated with her for over thirty years as dancer, choreographer, producer and artistic advisor, thus having first-hand knowledge of what she had to contend against, and of her unique achievement.

Conviction, dedication and passion are the fuels that propel into excellence, and Joan had these in abundance. She started her work for dance at a time when Ireland was impoverished, with scant financial resources for the arts. Yet she had the courage (some thought it foolhardiness) to embark on an extraordinary quest: to bring ballet to people all over the country – the classics, contemporary dance and new works created for her professional company. She was determined to see dance recognised as an essential element of Irish cultural life; she never wavered and never gave up.

She was a voyager, a discoverer of new worlds, many of her fine ballets being inspired by her country's beautiful cultural heritage of dance and story. She took generations of students with her into these realms, inspiring them to believe in themselves, adding colour to their lives and giving them the surety that they would succeed. She gave them a wider spectrum of how to look at the world and, through her example, demonstrated that, in spite of adversity, one can achieve the seemingly impossible. She had the great gift of being able to impart her love of her art to others, and win their support for the cause.

Jean Paul Sartre said: 'Man is not the sum of what he has, but the totality of what he does not yet have, or what he might have'. Joan Denise Moriarty's dream has yet to be fulfilled. It is good to see her memory being honoured, her example followed, and her life's work continued.

I had the privilege of her friendship, and remain to this day personally inspired by her artistry and work ethics. She was a woman of intrepid spirit and fortitude of whom Ireland can be proud.

Domy Reiter-Soffer, Joan Denise Moriarty at a meeting in 1975

Domy Reiter-Soffer, director, choreographer, artist, began his career with Israel Ballet; in 1962 he became a member of Irish Theatre Ballet, Ireland's first professional ballet company; from 1975-1989 he was choreographer and artistic advisor of Irish National Ballet. He has choreographed for television and film; he has created 25 ballets for the Bat-Dor Dance Company of Tel Aviv and recently three full-length ballets for Hong Kong Ballet. He works frequently in the United States with such companies as the Dance Theatre of Harlem, Louisville Ballet, Ohio Ballet; in 2010 Colorado Ballet performed his *Beauty and the Beast*. His *Pomes Penyeach*, *Yerma*, *Women*, and *Oscar* – Irish National Ballet's requiem – will long be remembered by ballet lovers in Ireland.

Domy has created multi-media theatrical productions, directed musicals (including the very successful *Mary Makebelieve* in Dublin's Abbey Theatre) and produced stage designs for over 30 productions, amongst others in La Scala Milan, the Dance Theatre of Harlem and Australian Ballet. He has had 22 one-man exhibitions of his paintings all over the world.

His website – http://domyrs.com/ – provides a wealth of documentation of his work.

A Life for Dance in Ireland

Ruth Fleischmann

Joan Denise Moriarty was the central figure of ballet in Ireland for a quarter of a century. The dancer, musician, teacher, choreographer founded the country's first professional ballet company in Cork in 1959. For in all 21 years her professional dancers toured Ireland, bringing the classics, contemporary ballet and her own original Irish choreography all over the country. Nothing like it had been attempted before, nor has anything similar been done since.

Little is known of her early life. She was brought up in England, her family having left Mallow around 1910. She studied ballet with Marie Rambert up to her early teens. When the family moved to Liverpool she may have continued with a relative, a member of the Royal Academy of Dancing who had a ballet school there. The earliest surviving documents show that the family was living in Liverpool from 1930. The Moriarties cherished their Irish roots. The boys were in the Gaelic Athletic Association and excellent hurlers; Joan was a member of the Gaelic League, an accomplished prize-winning warpiper and in 1931 champion Irish step-dancer of Britain.

The family returned to Mallow in the autumn of 1933, where Joan began to teach dance; after her mother's death, she moved to Cork in November 1940 to set up a school of dance there. It was not yet two decades since the end of the civil war, the majority of the population in the newly independent nation were small farmers, poverty was endemic, emigration or joining the British army in the war a necessity for hundreds of thousands. The system of education was conservative, firmly controlled by the Catholic church, examination-focused and not designed to nurture creativity and inspire innovation. The arts had no place in the curriculum. In 1940 the capital city had no professional orchestra, no opera company; no concert hall; the National Museum had a staff of two. Apart from Dublin's Abbey Theatre, the government did not fund the arts. It did, however, place them under surveillance: many of the best works of Ireland's writers fell foul of the Censorship Board and were banned on grounds of indecency or immorality.

That finding students and creating an audience for ballet was going

Above:
Moriarty champion piper,
Irish Press, April 25, 1934.

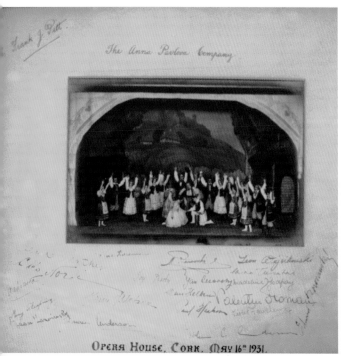

From top: Anna Pavlova Company in Cork.
This specially framed photograph, signed by the dancers, was presented to Frank Pitt, manager of the Opera House, by the Anna Pavlova Company in 1931 during their visit to Cork. It was given to Joan Denise Moriarty in 1951 by his successor.

Joan Denise Moriarty with Mallow pupils, 1935.

to be difficult under such conditions, goes without saying. Dublin saw ballet put on by occasional visiting groups and by its two dance companies. When in 1931 the Pavlova Company came to Cork, it was denounced in a Catholic church of the city and played to empty houses for a week. Moriarty came in for similar opprobrium twenty years later, her company's Opera House performance being described in a sermon as scandalous and offending against all normal codes of decency. But she was not intimidated and neither was the circle of ballet enthusiasts she had by then built up.

After taking up residence in Ireland, she continued to perform as an Irish dancer and piper; following a war pipes broadcast in 1938, she was invited by Sean Neeson to perform at a summer school for primary teachers in the Music Department of University College Cork. When the professor of music, Aloys Fleischmann, asked her to play the war pipes in a new composition of his in 1945, she agreed on condition that his symphony orchestra would accompany the ballet company she was planning to found. Thus began a unique collaboration which was to last for over 45 years and a friendship with three generations of Fleischmanns.

Moriarty developed a plan of campaign in the mid-1940s to make ballet a permanent part of Irish cultural life. It was to include a specifically Irish form of ballet, with original choreography inspired by the Gaelic heritage, and music commissioned from Irish composers. Ireland was to have a professional company which would tour the country, and a national academy of dance to train the best talent for it. Moriarty pursued this plan single-mindedly up to the end of her life, undeterred by hostility, indifference, lack of facilities and of finance, and managed to achieve it to an astonishing extent.

As a first step, the progress of her dance students allowed her to set up an amateur company in 1947; then, within ten years, the Cork

Ballet Company appeared with distinguished guest artists in the annual Ballet Week in performances of the great classical ballets. In 1951 the Arts Council of Ireland was established, albeit with a small budget and limited range of activity. By September 1959, Moriarty had her first major success with her plan to develop ballet in the urban centres and bring it from there into the small towns of Ireland. Having won sufficient support from the Arts Council, Gulbenkian Fund and the business world, she founded the first Irish full-time professional ballet company, Irish Theatre Ballet. It gave its premiere in Cork in December 1959 in the presence of its patron, Marie Rambert. During its first year the company performed in 70 towns across the

Left:
Moriarty, Fleischmann after the performance of his *Clare's Dragoons*, 1945.
Right:
Cork Symphony Orchestra rehearsal of
Clare's Dragoons, 1957.

Left:
Moriarty Cork
School, tap-dance class,
1940s.

13

Moriarty the dancer

country, under conditions which only young people fired by the enthusiasm of their director could have endured. But funding remained inadequate and precarious.

In Dublin in 1959 Patricia Ryan founded her amateur company, National Ballet; it had developed out of the National Ballet School, opened in 1953, which she had taken over in 1956. In 1961 she unionised the company; in 1962 registered it as professional. In 1963 the Arts Council insisted on a merger with Irish Theatre Ballet. However, after one season ending with performances in Cork in January 1964, it became evident that the financial and administrative problems were unsurmountable and in March 1964 the venture had to be given up.[1]

Ryan left Ireland; Moriarty continued her quest. She intensified her work with the Cork Ballet Company, and set out to create a wider basis for a professional company by increasing the number of dance schools in Munster. From 1970 the Cork Ballet Company began to perform every season in Dublin with such success that Moriarty's second professional company was established in 1973 with a government and subsequently Arts Council grant. Its patron Ninette de Valois donated half her Erasmus prize money to the new company, having attended and approved of the first performance. The Irish Ballet Company (later re-named Irish National Ballet) toured the country, north and south, for 16 years, often featuring on national television. Moriarty's ballet *The Playboy of the Western World* was performed in Belfast, Cork, Dublin, London, New York and Rennes; in

Left:
Moriarty ballet students
of the early years

Working with the Cork Ballet Company in later years

1979 she was awarded an honorary doctorate from the National University of Ireland for her services to dance in Ireland. That year the Arts Council purchased a historic Cork building, the Firkin Crane, to be restored as a home for the professional company and ultimately for a national dance academy.

In the mid 1980s, the Irish economy was in severe recession and government funding to the arts significantly reduced. During that time, the Arts Council developed new policies on dance; Moriarty resigned in 1985. Arts Council funding was withdrawn from Irish National Ballet in 1988; the following year the company had to be disbanded. Moriarty did not live to see the Firkin Crane building open as Cork's Dance Centre, having passed away on 24 January 1992.

This remarkable woman had battled all her life against every obstacle to establish ballet in Ireland on a permanent, professional footing. It was her love of the arts that made her determined to bring their richness into the lives of ordinary people. Her ability to impart her passion for dance to others inspired her students, her dancers, and the artists and friends without whose support she could not have achieved what she did. Her dignity and courage during the last years of her life awed those close to her when, her health failing, she had to cope with the tragedy of seeing professional ballet destroyed in Ireland.

Clockwise from top left: Moriarty with Ninette de Valois, Abbey Theatre Dublin, 1978. Cork Ballet Company board received at City Hall Cork by Lord Mayor Cllr. Frank Nash, July, 1991. Receiving the Variety Artists Trust Society award, Mansion House, Dublin, 1983. Guest of honour at 'This Is Your Life', 1988.

Ruth Fleischmann, born and educated in Cork, lectured in the English Department of the University of Bielefeld / Germany up to her retirement in 2007. She has published a study of the novelist Canon Sheehan, a biography of her musician grandfather, has documented aspects of her father's work for music and that of Joan Denise Moriarty for dance in Ireland.

1   See Patrick Zuk, *A.J. Potter (1918-1980)*, University of Durham Ph.D. thesis, 2008, Chapter 5; Norris Davidson's article in *Dance and Dancers* Jan 1961; Fay Weldon's article in *The Dancing Times* of June 1964 and the programme for the Cork season of Jan 1964.

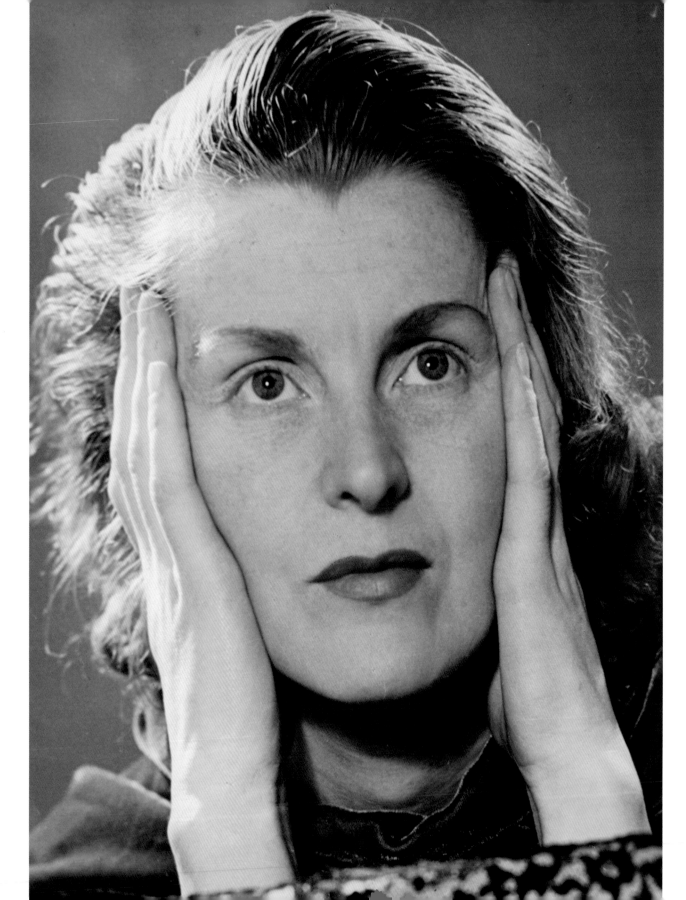

The Cork Ballet Company:
A Brief History

Monica Gavin

June 1st, 1947, was an auspicious date for the arts in Cork when the inaugural performance of Joan Denise Moriarty's Cork Ballet Group, accompanied by the Cork Symphony Orchestra, conducted by Professor Aloys Fleischmann, took place at the Opera House. The programme consisted of short ballets, choreographed by Miss Moriarty, to music by Schubert, Brahms, Stravinsky, Smetana and a solo, *La Calinda*, from the Delius opera *Koanga*, danced by Miss Moriarty. The press reported that the performance exceeded all expectations. Mr P. J. Little, Minister for Post and Telegraphs, in his address to the audience, reported in *The Irish Press*, said that the standard was astonishingly good. *The Cork Examiner*, in May 1948, announced a week of ballet at the Opera House with the Cork Symphony Orchestra, an association which continued until 1993.

A new class for business girls produced a number of enthusiastic would-be dancers. A strategic move in 1953 to a spacious studio at 1B Emmet Place, opposite the Opera House, was ideal for the future of the group, which in 1954 became Cork Ballet Company.

The following years continued with the pattern of short ballets which allowed the choreographer to include juniors from the school and seniors from the company in the productions from which evolved an adaptable *corps de ballet* and a number of top-class soloists and character dancers, such as Patricia O'Gorman and Hilda Buckley. Miss Moriarty choreographed over 100 works, many of which were based on Irish myths and legends, folk tales and customs, using traditional Irish dance steps and rhythms and incorporating classical movements to give them a dramatic quality. Suitable music was found in works by Irish composers.

The three act ballet *Coppélia*, re-produced by Miss Moriarty, was performed in Ballet Week 1955, and was attended by President Seán T. O' Kelly and his wife, who met the cast backstage and congratulated everyone on the production. A disastrous fire gutted the Opera House in December 1955 and the company moved to the City Hall for a number of years.

Right: After the Cork Ballet
Group's first performance, 1947.

(front l to r:)
Joan Denise Moriarty, *founder
of the Cork Ballet Group*;
P. J. Little, *Minister of Post
and Telegraphs*; Mrs Little;
Aloys Fleischmann, *composer,
conductor of the Cork
Symphony Orchestra*

(back l to r:)
Charles Lynch, *pianist*;
E.J. Moeran, *composer*;
Noreen O'Sullivan, *Cork
Orchestral Society*;
Marshall Hutson, *stage,
costume and programme
designer* and
Éamon O'Neill, *T.D.*

Polovtsian Dances,
Cork Ballet Group and choir,
1948.

In 1956 guest producer and dancer Peter Darrell and Domini Callaghan
were invited to present the company in *Swan Lake* Act 2 with full *corps de
ballet*. The programme also included *The Seal Woman* (music by Harty)
and a clever fun-filled circus *The Big Top* (Rossini) by Miss Moriarty. It was
a great success. The 1957 / 1958 seasons were a major step forward with
the production by Michel de Lutry of *Giselle* (Miss Moriarty danced the
part of Myrtha) and a really spectacular *Sleeping Princess*. He and his wife
Domini Callaghan and guests danced the principal parts and the company
provided the *corps de ballet*, with décor by M.C. Hutson and costumes by
his wife Clare. Stanley Judson, guest choreographer, produced *Les Sylphides*

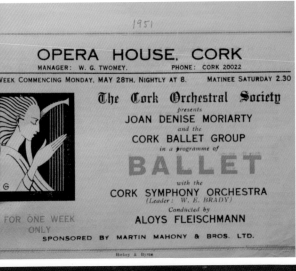

in 1959 and *La fille mal gardée* in 1960. Marina Svetlova and Kenneth Melville guested in both. *Les Sylphides* was also performed by Cork Ballet Company in 1965 for the gala opening, by President Éamon de Valera, of the new Cork Opera House.

Cinderella with soloists Joahne O'Hara, Domy Reiter-Soffer and John Cunningham was a perfect ballet for Christmas 1962 at the City Hall. The performance of *Coppélia* in the 1970 season, in the Opera House, was repeated in the Abbey Theatre, Dublin in March 1971 for one night. Lavinia Anderson and Domy Reiter-Soffer danced the principal roles. It was well received by a capacity, discerning audience, starved of full-length ballets.

Clockwise from top left:
Programme, 1951.

Suite classique, 1951.

Giselle, reproduced by Michel de Lutry, 1957; Moriarty (2nd from left) as Myrtha, Queen of the Willis.

Cork Ballet Company principal dancers 1956.

Clockwise from top left:
Meeting the Sadler's Wells guest artists for
The Sleeping Princess, 1958.
Cork Ballet Company rehearsing
with Stanley Judson, 1961.
Giselle, Helen Starr, Alain Dubreuil, 1971

The result was an equally successful visit later that year with Helen Starr and Alain Dubreuil in *Giselle*. November 1972 was a highlight for ballet in Ireland. The combined Cork Symphony Orchestra and Cork Ballet Company completed a brilliant week of *Swan Lake* in the Opera House and then the show transferred to Dublin. A week-long stay at

Gaiety
Theatre
Dublin

Directors: Eamonn Andrews, Lorcan Bourke, Fred O'Donovan,
Dermod Cafferky, Tom Walsh & Joe Kearns

NOVEMBER 13th to 17th, 1973

CORK BALLET COMPANY

presents

The Nutcracker
and the
Golden Bell of Ko

10p

the Gaiety, to full houses, was the ultimate success. The principal dancers were Sandra Conley, Alain Dubreuil, Mary Hanf and Gerald Byrne; the ballet was produced by Helen Starr. The production was attended by the Taoiseach Jack Lynch and his wife Máirín, who were staunch supporters of the Cork Ballet Company. The final visit to Dublin, in 1973,

Top: Final word before the Opera House performance, Nov 1970. L to r: Moriarty, Madeline Gordon, Sean Cunningham, Julia Cotter, Lavinia Anderson, and Domy Reiter-Soffer
Left: Dublin's Abbey Theatre, Anne Walsh, Lavinia Anderson, Madeline Gordon, Julia Cotter, 1970.

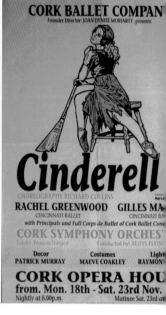

Patricia Crosbie,
"Cinderella" 1980.

CORK BALLET COMPAN
Founder Director: JOAN DENISE MORIARTY presents

Cinderell
CHOREOGRAPHY RICHARD COLLINS
RACHEL GREENWOOD   GILLES MA
CINCINNATI BALLET   CINCINNATI BA
with Principals and Full Corps de Ballet of Cork Ballet Comp
CORK SYMPHONY ORCHES
Leader: Frances Horgan   Conducted by: ALOYS FLEISC
Decor   Costumes   Light
PATRICK MURRAY   MAEVE COAKLEY   RAYMON
CORK OPERA HOU
from. Mon. 18th - Sat. 23rd Nov.
Nightly at 8.00p.m.   Matinee Sat. 23rd at

From left:
Cinderella,
Patricia Crosbie, 1980.

Opera House dressing room,
Nutcracker, 1990.

Poster for *Cinderella*, 1991.

was a first class *Nutcracker* with Helen Starr and Michel Bruel, produced by Alun Rys, which was attended by President Erskine Childers.

Highlights of the following years were *Petrouchka* with Domy Reiter-Soffer, *Scheherezade* with Julia Cotter and Richard Collins, both produced by Geoffrey Davidson, *La Sylphide* with Lavinia Anderson, Hilda Buckley and Babil Gandara, produced by Hans Brenna. In 1978 RTÉ 2 celebrated the gala opening at the Cork Opera House in which the company performed *The Sleeping Princess* Act 2 produced by Michel de Lutry, who also produced *Giselle* in 1982. In 1980 *Cinderella* was danced by Patricia Crosbie, partnered by Wayne Aspinall, produced by David Gordon. She also took the lead in *Swan Lake* and *Nutcracker*, produced by Richard Collins. The very popular Coleen Davis and Zoltan Solymosi danced with the company in *Swan Lake* and *The Sleeping Princess*.

Local musical and opera companies invited Miss Moriarty to provide dancers and to choreograph dance sequences for their productions. Among the popular shows were *Camelot*, *Finian's Rainbow*, *Guys and Dolls*, *The Wizard of Oz* and *My Fair Lady*. The operas included *Faust*, *La Traviata*, *Il Trovatore* and a highly successful three weeks of *Die Fledermaus*.

In 1957 the Irish Folk Dance Group of the Cork Ballet Company was formed to take part in the Cork International Choral and Folk Dance Festival as part of the new national festival, An Tóstal. The group toured to Germany and were prize winners in Dijon, France in 1961 and 1965. In October 1966 Ciarán MacMathúna introduced the first of thirteen Irish

CORK BALLET COMPANY
FOUNDER: JOAN DENISE MORIARTY
presents

Coppelia

CORK OPERA HOUSE
from Mon. 15th - Sat. 20th Nov., 1993

dance programmes given by the Cork Ballet Company on RTÉ. The half-hourly television series included *The Planting Stick*, *Straw Boys*, *Devil to Pay*, and the final production was *The Seal Woman*. The composers included Harty, Fleischmann, Ó Riada and Potter; the performing musicians Ceoltóirí Chualann and Na Filí.

The company won a number of critics' awards: Maeve Coakley for costumes, Ray Casey for lighting and Pat Murray for décor; the Brenda Last *Giselle* of 1992 won the Best Production award. It was a tribute to Dr. Joan Denise Moriarty and Professor Aloys Fleischmann, who both died earlier that year. President Mary Robinson attended the final night and met the cast backstage.

November 1993 saw the final performance of Cork Ballet Company with the three-act ballet *Coppélia* produced by Brenda Last. It was the end of a golden era.

From left:
Last meeting with Moriarty in the 'Grand Circle', 29 December 1991.

Cork Ballet Company's final production, 1993.

Monica Gavin was born and educated in Cork. She was a member of the Cork Ballet Company from 1954 to 1993. Since Moriarty's death in 1992, she has organised a series of exhibitions on her work for dance – in Firkin Crane Centre in 1997 to celebrate the 50th anniversary of the founding of the Company; in 2007 to commemorate CBC's 60th; in 2009 in Cork City Central Library, as well as in the Bishopstown, Mayfield and Wilton Libraries; and in 2010 as part of the Fleischmann centenary celebrations in the Firkin Crane.

From top, each row left to right:

Clare Hutson, Leslie Horne, CBC
Echo April 17, 1957.

Frank Sanquest, stage design painter,
exhibition with self-portrait.

Melba Foott, make-up for
Sally O'Neill.

Clare Hutson Folk costume designs.

1961 Clare Hutson Prisoners of the
Sea Mananán costume design.

Peer Gynt, Norah Ford-Kirkpatrick,
1949.

Rachel Burrows costume design.

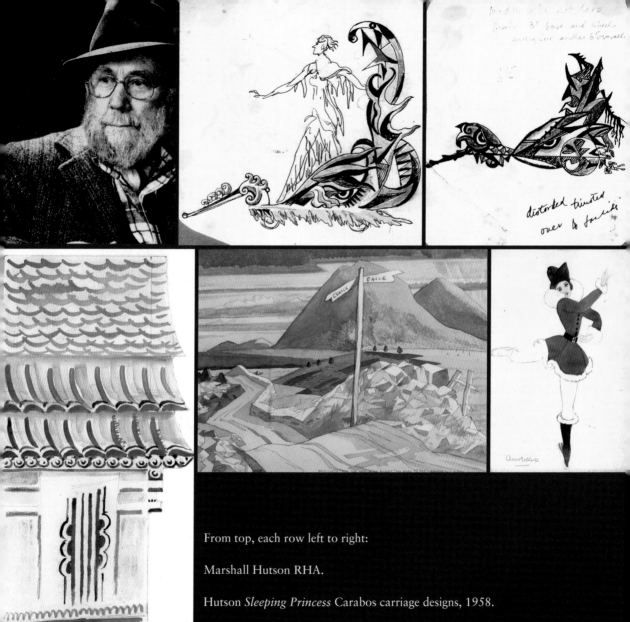

From top, each row left to right:

Marshall Hutson RHA.

Hutson *Sleeping Princess* Carabos carriage designs, 1958.

The Golden Bell of Ko design Marshall Hutson, 1948.

Devil to Pay, Hutson backdrop, 1962.

Clare Hutson costume design for *Carnaval des Glisseurs*, 1956.

Folk Dance Group of the Cork Ballet Company

Facing page, clockwise from top left: CBC Folk Dance Group. Folk Dance Group in France, 1961. International Festival in Germany, 1958.

Clockwise from top left: In Wewelsburg Castle, Germany, 1958. In Deidesheim Berlin, 1966. *An Damhsa* 13-part TV CBC dance series for RTÉ, 1966.

A Cork Lady's Dream Comes True

The Professional Companies:
Irish Theatre Ballet (1959-64),
Irish National Ballet (1973-89)

Patricia Crosbie

As a child I remember studying the framed newspaper article that proudly hung on the ballet studio wall at 1B Emmet Place: Joan Denise Moriarty sits proud and erect among a group of nine ballerinas. The headline reads 'A Cork Lady's Dream Comes True'. It referred to JDM's professional Irish Theatre Ballet Company (ITB), formed in Cork in 1959. The company, though small in number, was prolific in creativity and performances. JDM imported the talents of Stanley Judson, Geoffrey Davidson, Joahne O'Hara and Domy Reiter-Soffer (who later became artistic director and choreographer for Irish National Ballet) from abroad. Local dancers included Lavinia Anderson, Julia Cotter and Maureen Weldon, who were all trained by JDM, and Kay Mc Laughlin and Sean Cunningham, who both went on to dance with Irish National Ballet in the 1970s. Irish Theatre Ballet performed throughout Ireland, literally travelling the highways and byways bringing performances to many towns throughout the country, often accompanied by the world-renowned pianist, Charles Lynch. Its repertoire included JDM's signature Irish ballets, *Devil to Pay* and *West Cork Ballad*, her innovative *Prisoners of the Sea* and *Street Games*, and classics such as *Coppélia* and *Les Sylphides*. Unfortunately, with just a small grant from the Arts Council and wavering support from private sponsorship, ITB was soon in financial difficulties and sadly folded in 1964.

Nine years later JDM secured financial support from the government of the day, to form her new ballet company. This was Irish Ballet Company (re-named Irish National Ballet in 1983). As a student of JDM's ballet school in Cork, my own dream came true when I was offered a place with the professional company in 1976 and I was privileged and proud to dance with it until 1982. The opportunity to work with many internationally renowned

Left to right:

ITB ballet master
Stanley Judson, JDM,
manager Leslie Horne, 1959.

Francis of Assisi, 1962.

choreographers and teachers from the dance world laid the foundations of my career as a dancer and my identity as an Irish ballet dancer. These included Sir John Gilpin, Sir Anton Dolin, Peter Darrell, Michel de Lutry, David Gordon, Toni Beck, Rachel Cameron, Hans Brenaa, Richard Collins, Charles Czarny, Tony Hulbert, Royston Maldoom, Domy Reiter-Soffer, Flemming Ryberg and Brenda Last. With these choreographers in its credits, and under the patronage of Irish-born Dame Ninette de Valois, founder and artistic director of The Royal Ballet School and Company, JDM's ballet company flourished.

Dancers from all parts of the world, including America, UK, France, Iran, Finland, Holland and Ireland were employed on annual contracts. The company's international group of dancers remained small in number, fluctuating between sixteen and twenty-two dancers per year. This produced an unusual, eclectic and cosmopolitan microcosm living and working in Cork.

The company's repertoire was diverse and wide-ranging. It consisted of classical *pas de deux* extracted from the full length ballets, including *Le Corsaire, Don Quioxte, Black Swan, Flames of Paris, Sleeping Beauty* and *Cinderella*; contemporary and postmodern ballets specifically created for the company such as *Women, Paradise Gained, Adagietto, Shadow Reach* and *Brandenburg*; established ballets or divertissements including *La Ventana, Othello, Pas de Quatre, Raymonda* and *Laurencia*, and JDM's signature folk ballets danced to traditional Irish music such as *Billy the Music* and

Left:
Prisoners of the Sea,
with Julia Cotter, 1961.

The Playboy of the Western World. This mix of classical, contemporary and Irish folk ballets all contributed to the eclectic identity of the company that reflected the openness of its founder, JDM.

Along with annual seasons at Dublin's Abbey Theatre and Cork Opera House, the company toured Ireland every spring and autumn. Participation in both the Dublin and Wexford Opera Festivals ensured we reached a wider and more international audience. RTÉ's television broadcasts of various ballet performances brought a varied slice of the country's national dance company's repertoire into people's homes. Innovative and successful tours in war-torn Northern Ireland in the late 1970s and early 1980s were grant-aided by the Arts Council of Northern Ireland; the company received a warm welcome and great applause in towns such as Coleraine, Derry, Lisnaskea and Newry. Few companies visited the North in those difficult days: such cultural bridge-building was characteristic of the pioneering influence of JDM on dance in the whole of Ireland. A short tour of the then Yugoslavia had brought the company to cross another divide in 1977.

When commissioned in 1978 to create a ballet for the Dublin Theatre Festival, JDM choreographed her memorable folk ballet, *The Playboy of the Western World,* based on John Millington Synge's play of the same name. *Playboy,* with the live accompaniment of the traditional Irish music group *The Chieftains,* took the company out of Ireland to perform abroad, securing performances in New York's City Center Theatre in 1979, London's Sadler's Wells Theatre in 1980 and Rennes in 1984. This was a

From top:
ITB in Belfast,
ballet master Geoffrey
Davidson, JDM, dancers,
1962.

Northern Ireland tour,
January, 1962.

personal triumph for JDM and her dream was growing. In 1981, again at the request of the Dublin Theatre Festival, she choreographed her second full length ballet, *The Táin,* for the company. Based on Irish mythology, this ballet was premiered at the Olympia Theatre, Dublin with the RTÉ Symphony Orchestra playing Aloys Fleischmann's specially commissioned score. Both these ballets, *Playboy* and *Táin,* were unique and original and were undoubtedly the forerunners of *Riverdance,* placing JDM securely at the forefront of Irish dance.

However, dark days for dance and the arts in Ireland were looming by the mid-1980's. A reduction in the finances distributed to the arts came in the wake of serious economic problems besetting the country as a whole. For reasons too numerous to mention here, JDM sadly resigned as artistic director in 1985. With her went the company's identity and its director's dream. In 1988 the Arts Council withdrew its grant. In spite of a valiant effort by Domy Reiter-Soffer and Patrick Murray to rescue the company with a production of the critically-acclaimed new ballet *Oscar* by Reiter-Soffer, no further funding was forthcoming. In 1989 Irish National Ballet had to be disbanded. JDM's dream was over.

Joan Denise Moriarty's stalwart pioneering for professional dance in the face of apathy was truly inspirational. She offered a glimpse of beauty, creativity and entertainment to audiences across the country. By achieving her dream all those years ago, JDM also gave dreams and hopes to so many children, students, dancers and creators of professional dance. From one Cork lady to another, I salute you Miss Moriarty in the year of your centenary, and humbly thank you for helping me to achieve truth in my own dream.

Patricia Crosbie was born in Cork and commenced her early dance training in the Joan Denise Moriarty School of Dance. A member of Irish National Ballet for six years, she then moved to London where she worked with many companies and choreographers, travelling all over the world. Patricia is Ballet Mistress with Cork City Ballet and teaches the Diploma in Dance course at Coláiste Stiofán Naofa. She was awarded an MA in Dance at the University of Limerick, where she is now ballet teacher at the Irish World Academy of Music and Dance.

Above:
The merged company, JDM, Patricia Ryan, Dublin curtain call, November 1963.

Below:
Patricia Crosbie

Moriarty / Ó Riada - *Devil to Pay*

Images from *Devil to Pay*. Eoinín: Richard Collins, his wife: Anna Donovan, beggar girl: Carol Bryans, Irish Ballet Company 1978.

Letter from the composer, Séan Ó Riada: fees given in Moriarty's hand.

Crosbie Irish National Ballet

Clockwise from top left: Irish Ballet Company, 1974. IBC 1st performance, de Valois congratulating the dancers, 1974. Domy Reiter-Soffer, choreographer, artistic advisor. His ballet *Women,* 1974.

Crosbie Irish
National Ballet

Clockwise from top left: *Billy the Music*, 1974. Northern Irish tour, Portstewart, 1979. JDM RTÉ
TV commission, *Reputations*. *Pomes Penyeach*, Jonathan Burnett, Wayne Aspinall, Diane Grey,
1982. *Oscar* Cork Opera House, 1989. *Playboy of the Western World* in Rennes, France, 1984.
Playboy in New York, 1979. *Playboy of the Western World*, Sean Cunningham, Anna Donovan

Crosbie Irish National Ballet

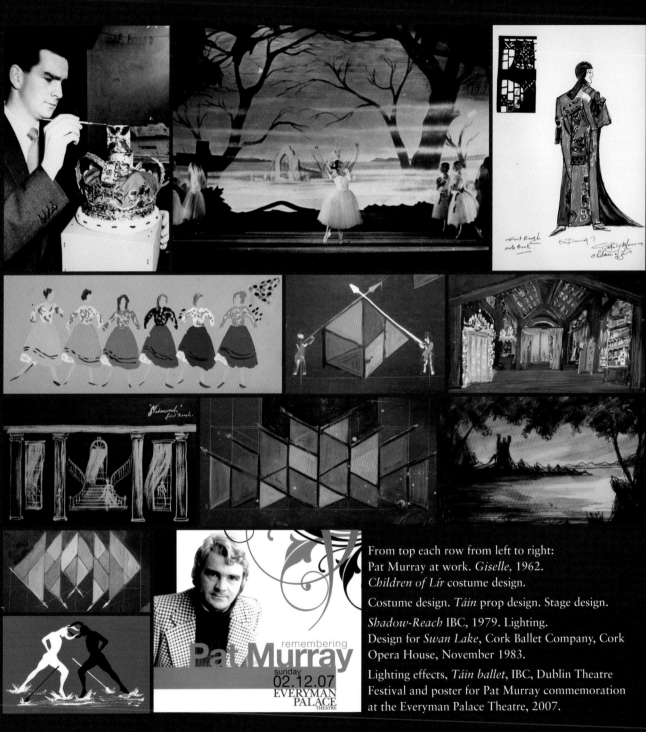

From top each row from left to right:
Pat Murray at work. *Giselle*, 1962.
Children of Lír costume design.

Costume design. *Táin* prop design. Stage design.

Shadow-Reach IBC, 1979. Lighting.
Design for *Swan Lake*, Cork Ballet Company, Cork
Opera House, November 1983.

Lighting effects, *Táin ballet*, IBC, Dublin Theatre
Festival and poster for Pat Murray commemoration
at the Everyman Palace Theatre, 2007.

Joan Denise Moriarty's **Irish Theatre Ballet,** Patricia Ryan's **National Ballet** merged as **Irish National Ballet** Sep 1963-March 1964

Facing page, from top: Patricia Ryan, *Caitlín Bocht*, Dublin Olympia Theatre Nov 1963.
Ester Ó Brolchain, *Saudacáo a America*, Dublin Olympia Theatre Nov 1963.
This page: Moriarty, *Prisoners of the Sea*, Dublin Olympia Theatre Nov 1963

What's in a Step?
Moments in the Choreographic
Language of Joan Denise Moriarty

David Wallace

Joan Denise Moriarty was one of the most important figures in dance in Ireland during the latter part of the twentieth century. She pioneered dance in education and through the setting up of her professional companies and the amateur Cork Ballet Company she sought to make dance an integral part of the Irish cultural scene. Throughout her career she strived to create a uniquely Irish utterance of ballet and in many of her own works explored Irish themes, myths and legends.

The most interesting and remarkable aspect of Moriarty's choreography is its musicality. Of course, as she was a musician, this should come as no surprise, but in the world of dance a choreographer who understands the working of musical phrases and can play with the music on a technical level to create a counterpoint is rare indeed – Balanchine comes to mind here. Her choreographic notebooks demonstrate that she worked closely with the music and favoured working with minutage – timings according to minutes and seconds rather than actual scores – especially when working with traditional music. This of course would have been preferable as there was probably no score available of the tunes. Her notebooks with scores highlight bar numbers and work closely to the given time signatures, sometimes creating a counterpoint by giving the dancers different counts to that in the score. *The Táin* (Moriarty/Fleischmann 1981) provides fascinating evidence of counterpoint between dance and music and a host of other aspects.[1] The movement vocabulary she uses is heavily influenced by ballet with interjections from the Irish tradition; depending on the subject matter of the ballet she includes steps such as tipping and battery, jig steps and reel steps – particularly the travelling steps. She has a penchant for dramatic gesture and deploys this to great effect in ballets such as *Lugh of the Golden Arm* and *Playboy of the Western World* (Moriarty/Chieftains 1978). She uses the stage space well and often her crowd scenes are the

Left:
Seán Ó Riada
(Courtesy T. Ó Canainn)

Right:
Ceoltóirí Chualann
rehearsing

most fascinating to watch as the layers of character and drama are cleverly arranged. One often gets the sense of fragility when watching the solo choreography; she favours simple steps and clear lines that, for the most part, give her the vocabulary she requires to create.

I would like to focus on the ballet *Lugh of the Golden Arm* and to discuss in some detail a few moments from this work. The ballet was created in 1977 for Moriarty's professional company, the Irish Ballet Company, to music by Seán Ó Riada and Éamon de Buitléar, performed by Ceoltóirí Chualann and Ceoltóirí Laighean. It was broadcast by RTÉ in March of that year; the dancers were: Babil Gandara, Richard Collins, Carol Bryans, Patricia Crosbie, Eileen Barry and Margaret Goodner.[2]

Lugh was the Mercury of the Celtic gods – light-footed, nimble, skilled in crafts and an inventor, he was a protector and champion of the downtrodden. In the story of this ballet he comes to the aid of a young widow, Fidelma of the Long Hair, whose husband has been murdered by a warrior of an invading clan. With mourners bearing his sword, shield and cloak, she laments his death. When the warrior bursts in to kill her too, Lugh appears and in single combat defeats the warrior. Fidelma dances in thanksgiving for her deliverance; she folds her husband's cloak, and as she does so, the burden of her grief is eased, for his dying request has been granted – he has been avenged.[3]

In the choreography there is a fusion of Irish traditional steps with those from the lexicon of the ballet. This is particularly evident in the choreography for Babil Gandara, a dancer of considerable skill, sharp footwork and impressive elevation. *Lugh of the Golden Arm* very

successfully showcases his talents: the battle scene between Lugh and the Invading Warrior is an exciting mix of grand allegro and allegro steps paired with dramatic gestures, free movement and steps from the Irish tradition. His solo before the mourners come onstage is characteristically *brilliante* and virtuoso, conveying the mischievous nature of Lugh. Some of the most interesting movement material is reserved for the three mourners and Fidelma of the Long Hair. This material creates a striking contrast with the allegro steps executed by Gandara. Here we see Moriarty's skill in creating dramatic tension onstage. Much of the material for the three

Clockwise from top left:
Lugh of the Golden Arm, 1977, Babil Gandara

Babil Gandara and Richard Collins

Anna Donovan as Fidelma

Babil Gandara and Richard Collins

Above:
Carol Bryans as Fidelma,
Lugh of the Golden Arm
(© RTÉ Stills Library)

mourning women and Fidelma of the Long Hair is striking because of its stark and bleak nature. I was reminded here of Bronislava Nijinska's *Les Noces*, the ballet to Stravinsky's music based on Russian peasant wedding customs[4], particularly the material from the bride's dressing scene, where the *pointe* shoe is used in a stabbing motion with a marked downward accent, the angst of the women articulated by this most feminine aspect of ballet. In *Lugh*, the sideways glances with expressionless faces and the tableau held for a few moments each time also have echoes of Nijinska's vocabulary. Bleakness is the most striking tone that comes across. As in *Les*

Above:
Lugh of the Golden Arm,
the mourners Patricia
Crosbie, Eileen Barry and
Margaret Goodner.

Noces, the lack of facial expression and the carefully contained upper body create a sense of unease, of course the two contexts are completely different and perhaps this is a more obvious context to have such movement, but it is just as effective.

Legs and feet only tell half the story in any choreographic work. The upper bodies of these women are twisted and contorted within the chest space, and the arms further accent this: they seem to reach out into the air as if to seize something that is not there, searching and reaching. Sometimes the arms are contained across the chest, fist over the heart with the head turned away as if compelled by the force of their grief to avert their eyes from the onlookers. There is a sense in this part of the choreography that this whole scene takes place under water or that the dancers are suspended in a thicker atmosphere. Their movements look heavy and laboured, especially with the appearance of Fidelma after the mourners. The inclusion of the cloak, shield and sword brings our attention to the function of these women in depicting the death-theme of the ballet. The cloak is used to extend the space of the dancer using wide sweeps low on the floor to mark circles in an almost ritualistic way.

47

West Cork Ballad,
Irish Ballet Company
1974, (left to right:)
Melanie Morgan,
Rosemary Stacey,
Wendy Albrow,
Monica Johanneson and
Domy Reiter-Soffer.

In terms of use of space Moriarty keeps the four women in close proximity to each other, once they are all on stage. They weave around each other creating tension within the space between them. They are never allowed to venture more than an arm's length from each other; we get the impression that if they did they would dissolve into some mystic ether that surrounds them. Once the mourners have left the stage Fidelma begins to dance her lament. Accompanied by harp she weaves around the stage stopping in various arabesque poses, again stretching out from her chest space, but still always contained within, this suggested by the cloak in which she envelopes herself. She moves cautiously around the stage and wraps herself in the cloak as if to further highlight her inward angst. Her hands are used to frame her face in various ways, highlighting the expressionless face during moments of stillness in the ballet. In contrast, the space for the two male dancers is expanded to include the whole stage. The use of travelling steps, many from the Irish tradition, and wide leaps facilitate this expansion. Everything here seems grounded and real, the space is covered, there are very few spaces for us to imagine; the space is fully articulated by the dancers.

Moriarty's response to both the music and the subject matter of the ballet is apt and effective. It demonstrates a choreographer of skill and intelligence especially where music and drama are concerned. In ballet much emphasis is put on the steps: on getting them right, higher, sharper, quicker; what Moriarty does in her work is challenge us to look beyond the steps, to look into the movement and see the character. This is not to say that the

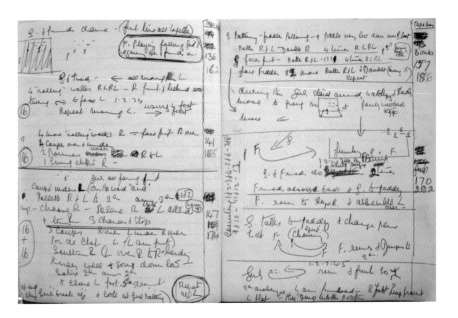

A section from the notebook for *West Cork Ballad* (Moriarty/Ó Riada, 1961). The tape recording numbers are in the right margin indicating precise minutes corresponding to steps written in the centre. Both ballet and Irish steps can be discerned.

movement is unimportant, on the contrary it is highly effective and skilled choreography suited to its purpose.

Of course these are but moments in the very large output of Joan Denise Moriarty, but they allow us to imagine what treasures lie in store for those who are willing to explore a most fascinating period in Irish cultural history.

David Wallace is a native of Kilkenny. He holds a B.Mus.degree from Cork CIT School of Music. He studied composition with Rhona Clarke and Séamas de Barra; he has a MMus from the London Guildhall School of Music and Drama and an PGDip in Dance from Roehampton University, London. He is planning to do a Ph.D. on the choreography of Joan Denise Moriarty's Irish ballets.

David Wallace

1   I gave a paper on this subject, *Joan Denise Moriarty and Aloys Fleischmann – The Music and the Dance*, at The First International Conference of Irish Music and Musicians at Durham University in July 2010. The paper presented a choreomusical analysis of the Camp Maidens' Dance from the ballet *The Táin*.

2   I would like to thank Ray Casey for allowing me access to his video and DVD collection, among which is the RTÉ recording of *Lugh of the Golden Arm*, broadcast as part of the Folio series in March 1977.

3   The outline is based on the programme note of the Irish Ballet Company's 7th season, which began at the Cork Opera House on 4th Feb 1980.

4   *Les Noces* was originally commissioned by Diaghilev for his Ballets Russes in 1913, and was to have been choreographed by Nijinsky, but it was first staged in 1923, with choreography by Nijinsky's sister, Bronislava.

Joan Denise Moriarty and the Music for the Ballet

Séamas de Barra

Although it was presented for one evening only, The Cork Ballet Group's first production in June 1947 was so successful that Moriarty and Fleischmann were emboldened to risk a more ambitious undertaking the following year. Not only did they intend to stage a full week of ballet in 1948, but they also courageously decided to introduce two new Irish works to Cork audiences. The first of these, *Puck Fair*, had a scenario by F. R. Higgins and music by Elizabeth Maconchy, an English-born composer with strong Irish connections who was now rapidly making a name for herself in England. *Puck Fair* had already been staged in Dublin in 1941 in a version with two pianos, but for the Cork production the score was orchestrated by Ina Boyle and new choreography devised by Moriarty. The second work in the 1948 programme, a ballet on a Chinese theme entitled *The Golden Bell of Ko*, was the first of several vivid scores that Fleischmann composed for Moriarty over the next few years.

Thus from the beginning Moriarty instituted a policy of engaging with the work of contemporary Irish composers. The Cork Ballet Group, however, barely covered the cost of staging its annual production and was not in a position to offer commissioning fees for new scores. Fleischmann, recognising the cultural importance of Moriarty's enterprise, gave it his full support both practically, by making the Cork Symphony Orchestra available for the annual ballet week and, creatively, by his willingness to compose new works without remuneration. But the same degree of altruism could not reasonably be expected of other composers. Nonetheless, given such slender financial resources, the early years were surprisingly rich in modern Irish ballets.

The Children of Lir, which was specially written for the Cork Ballet Group by the Derry composer Redmond Friel, was performed in 1950. Fleischmann composed his second ballet score, *An Cóitín Dearg* [The Red Petticoat], to a scenario by Micheál MacLiammóir for the 1951 season, and in 1952 *The Singer* (1935), an existing 'dance drama' by

Facing page:
The first page of the piano score of Fleischmann's *The Golden Bell of Ko*, extracted by Aloys Fleischmann senior from the orchestral score, with Moriarty's choreographic notes, 1948.

51

Left to right:
Joan Denise Moriarty

Fleischmann rehearsing
Aula Max UCC, Cork
Symphony Orchestra,
leader D. Foley

Cork Symphony Orchestra
rehearsal in the old Opera
House, leader W. Brady

Éamonn Ó Gallchobhair based on a story by Pádraig Pearse, was staged with new choreography by Moriarty. The 1952 season also saw the first collaboration between Moriarty and Fleischmann's student Seán Ó Riada (or John Reidy, as he was then known), who had just graduated from UCC. After Fleischmann's mother Tilly had programmed Schumann's *Papillons* in one of her recitals it occurred to her that it would make an excellent basis for a ballet. She devised a scenario that appealed to Moriarty, who agreed to choreograph it, and Ó Riada undertook to arrange the music for orchestra. This was the first of several ballets Moriarty would create with Ó Riada, who arguably became her most important musical collaborator after Fleischmann.

The Golden Bell of Ko was revived in 1953 and the following year another existing work by Ó Gallchobhair, *Casadh an tSúgáin* [The Twisting of the Rope] (1939) was produced. By 1955, with eight years of successful productions behind her, Moriarty decided that the Cork Ballet Company (as it had now become) should attempt for the first time a full-length ballet from the standard repertoire. Delibes' *Coppélia* was chosen. It was decided to pair it in a double bill with another new Fleischmann ballet, *Macha Ruadh* [Red-haired Macha], which in the opinion of the press was the most successful new work yet presented. This was the last important score Fleischmann composed for The Cork Ballet Company apart from *Bata na bPlanndála* [The Planting Stick], a delightful short work written for performance during the 1957 Cork International Choral Festival by Moriarty's Folk Dance Group.

In 1953, Fleischmann approached A. J. Potter, a Belfast-born composer based in Dublin, to enquire if he had written any music that might be suitable

for adaptation as a ballet. Four years later, Potter's music was used in a satirical ballet depicting the dichotomy between tradition and modernity in Irish society. It was ironically entitled *Moy Mell*, an anglicisation of Magh Meala [The Plain of Honey] the imaginary Gaelic never-land, and the contemporary theme was tellingly conveyed by juxtaposing Potter's arrangements of Irish folk tunes and music by Gershwin. Fleischmann was only in a position to offer Potter an honorarium of ten guineas, which is a clear indication of how modest the resources of the Cork Ballet Company were: 'I realise how inadequate this is', he wrote apologetically, 'but we are always in financial difficulties and penury has become second nature!'

Potter subsequently became closely associated with the founding of Patricia Ryan's professional National Ballet in Dublin in the early 1960s, for which he composed three scores in quick succession, the third of which, *Caitlín Bhocht* [Poor Cathleen], was also performed in Cork in 1964 by Irish National Ballet (an amalgamation of National Ballet and Moriarty's professional Irish Theatre Ballet) and the Cork Ballet Company. But his most important collaboration with Moriarty did not take place until over a

Potter's *Moy Mell* with Mary O'Callaghan, Maurice McCarthy, Cherry Hutson and Declan O'Riordan, 1957.

From top: Gaiety, *Golden Bell of Ko*, Hilda Buckley, Michael Glendinning, 1973.

Full Moon for the Bride, 1974.

The Chieftains, 1978.

decade later when in 1974 she staged his *Full Moon for the Bride*.

The idea for this ballet dates from 1959 when Micheál MacLiammóir approached Potter to compose music for a scenario of his own devising. Potter duly completed the work in the form of a piano score, but MacLiammóir's attempts to secure a production at that time came to nothing and there seemed little prospect of it receiving a performance in Ireland once the Dublin-based National Ballet was disbanded in 1964. There the matter rested until 1972 when the Cork Ballet Company took its production of Tchaikovsky's *Swan Lake* to Dublin. Mac Liammóir, who saw the production and was deeply impressed, asked Moriarty if she would choreograph and produce *Full Moon for the Bride*. Initially reluctant, Potter eventually agreed to orchestrate the score, although he demanded to be paid at current union rates for the job which put the Company under severe additional financial strain. The Cork Ballet Company made a second visit to the capital in 1973 (with Tchaikovsky's *Nutcracker* and a second revival of *The Golden Bell of Ko*) and on its third visit the following year it presented Adam's *Giselle* and the Potter-MacLiammóir ballet. While these three successive seasons in Cork and Dublin were undoubtedly successful from the artistic point view, all the productions incurred heavy losses. The level of official interest they aroused, however, led directly to the establishment of the professional Irish Ballet Company (later, Irish National Ballet) in 1974.

Although short-lived, Moriarty's professional Irish Theatre Ballet (1959-1964) also produced a number of ballets to scores by contemporary Irish composers. In 1960, the Cork composer Bernard Geary, who had been a student of Fleischmann's at UCC in the 1950s, wrote two short works, *Bitter Aloes* and *Il Cassone* (which were choreographed by Geoffrey Davidson), and in 1961 Moriarty resumed her collaboration with Seán Ó Riada, who provided a folk-music based score for *West Cork Ballad*. This proved so successful that the following year Ó Riada was asked to devise a similar score for a second folk ballet, *The Devil to Pay*.

Disappointment at the demise of Irish Theatre Ballet gave way to renewed hope for dance in Ireland when the professional Irish Ballet Company was set up. The inaugural season in 1974 featured a third folk ballet to music by Ó Riada (who had died three years previously), *Billy the Music,* which allowed Moriarty to showcase her own distinctive choreographic style based on an individual fusion of Irish folk dance and ballet steps. One further ballet using Ó Riada's music, *Lugh of the Golden Arm*, was produced in 1977. With its combination of Irish traditional music and Irish mythology, this seemed to prefigure the next two works Moriarty

Playboy, Sean Cunningham as Christy, 1978.

Táin,
Patricia Crosbie and
Roger Wade, 1981.

created for the Irish National Ballet, and which in some respects represent the apex of her career as a choreographer. The first of these was *The Playboy of the Western World* (1978), an elaborate piece in the folk style based on the play by John Millington Synge. It was choreographed to arrangements of traditional music performed by *The Chieftains*, a popular ensemble founded in 1962 following Ó Riada's pioneering Ceoltóirí Chualann.

After *The Playboy* had been danced triumphantly in London and New York, Moriarty and Fleischmann embarked on their last joint creative venture. This was *The Táin* (1981), a full-length ballet in three acts with a scenario adapted from Thomas Kinsella's translation of the *Táin Bó Cúailnge*. Fleischmann produced a new score for this choreographic version of the greatest of Irish legends about Cuchulainn and Queen Medb and the work was performed to widespread acclaim at the Dublin Theatre Festival in 1981.

The final contemporary score Moriarty called into being was for a ballet she planned in commemoration of the poet and revolutionary soldier, Pádraig Pearse, the centenary of whose birth was celebrated in 1979. On Fleischmann's advice, she approached the young Dublin composer John Buckley, who agreed to write the music. The idea was that the ballet would explore Pearse's dedicated patriotism in personal rather than political terms,

and was accordingly based on 'Fornocht do Chonac Thú' [Naked I Saw Thee] (the original title of Buckley's score), a poem in which he confronts the nature and consequences of his sacrifice. In the event, the ballet was not staged until 1983 under the title *Diúltú* [Renunciation]. Two years later the Brinson report was published and Moriarty resigned from Irish National Ballet. By 1989 Irish National Ballet had ceased to exist altogether. Moriarty continued to direct the Cork Ballet Company until her death in 1992, but she created no more works to music by Irish composers.

Left: Fleischmann at a rehearsal of *Swan Lake*, Cork Ballet Company, 1972 with Helen Starr and Sandra Conley.

Right: *Diúltú*, Carol Bryans, Wiley Gallaher and Anna Donovan, 1983.

Below: Séamas de Barra

Séamas de Barra, composer and musicologist, is a graduate of University College Cork. He is co-editor (with Patrick Zuk) of Field Day Music, an innovative series of monographs on Irish composers to which he contributed *Aloys Fleischmann* in 2006. He has published numerous articles on Irish music and is currently working on a study of the music of John Kinsella.

The Firkin Crane

.

Paul McCarthy

Cork's 'North Side' is defined by hills rising up from the north channel of the river Lee which retain the city's more hidden charms. A warren of tiny streets, many still cobbled, surround some magnificent buildings, leading visitors to wonderful views as they explore the Shandon area.

In this setting lies the Firkin Crane, a unique building where support is provided for every aspect of professional dance: space for individual artists to research and create; studios for personal and shared practice; administrative and technical facilities as well as two performance theatres.

Opened in August 1855, the original building was designed by Sir John Benson to meet the needs of the Butter Exchange. 'Firkin' is a Danish word meaning quarter-barrel, which represented nine gallons or eighty pounds of butter. In former times the tarred firkins or casks were weighed on a balance known as a 'crane', hence the name.

The Butter Market closed in 1924, but the dairy connection continued with the manufacture of margarine until the 1970's, when the building became vacant and was put up for sale.

In 1973, Joan Denise Moriarty founded the professional dance company, the Irish Ballet Company (later to be re-named Irish National Ballet), but had no suitable accommodation for it. In 1979 the Arts Council bought the Firkin Crane for the company. But in July 1980 the building was destroyed by fire and a huge sum was now required for the reconstruction.

A Trust Fund was set up by the Irish Ballet Company, with the former Taoiseach Jack Lynch as president. Cork City Council supported the undertaking as part of its plan to develop the whole Shandon area. The Lord Mayor travelled to Brussels to make a successful plea for European funding. Government monies followed, as did contributions from many Cork businesses and from the Irish American Fund. Planning started in 1982 with meticulous concern to address the needs of professional dance, while preserving a building of architectural interest in what is recognised as the

A fund-raising campaign will be launched shortly to enable restoration work to begin on the Company's premises at Shandon. The early 19th century Rotunda in what was once the "Liberties" of Cork was gutted by fire (pictured above), and it is hoped to rebuild it as a permanent home for Ireland's national dance company.

Clockwise from top left: Planning begins, 1981.

Fundraising begins.

Lord Mayor seeks funds for Firkin from Europe, 1982.

most historic part of Cork city. In 1984 the planners received a prestigious E.E.C. architectural award. Building began in 1985, the year in which the 800th anniversary of the granting of the city's charter was celebrated.

Ireland suffered a severe recession in the 1980s, in the course of which funding for the arts was greatly reduced. In 1989 Irish National Ballet had to be disbanded, a tragedy for Dr Moriarty and for Irish ballet. She did not live to see the Firkin Crane building completed, but she knew that it would be, and that it would become a centre for dance. The Firkin Crane opened in April 1992, three months after her death. Jack Lynch unveiled a sculpture of her there in tribute to the indomitable woman whose 'courage and culture' had made it possible.

The Firkin Crane today remains a centre dedicated to dance, serving Cork's growing dance community, its continuing involvement with groups, individuals and organisations in the city creating valuable social platforms.

Culture and courage led to lasting legacy

FORMER Taoiseach Jack Lynch last night paid tribute to the late Joan Denise Moriarty for her 'courage and culture' and her immense contribution to Ireland's cultural life.

Clockwise from top left: Jack Lynch pays tribute to Moriarty.

The Firkin Crane restored, 1992.

Moriarty's life summed up in an article from the *Cork Examiner,* October 1985.

Cork 800, October 1985

N this special interview with **TIM CRAMER,** the founder and ormer Artistic Director of the Irish National Ballet, DR. OAN DENISE MORIARTY, talks about her life as first lady f the dance in Ireland.

She dreamed an impossible dream

RK 800 is about a city and its history, its ditions, its pride, and above all, its people. One rson who has contributed greatly to that sense of de is Dr. Moriarty. This, encapsulated, is her ry. It needs no embroidery, no embellishment. As ale of courage, vision and determination, it speaks itself.

little girl of sat gazing into fire, as child-will do. There saw figures in flames, caves,

Meanwhile, she had to be up at 6.15 every morning to get to school at the Convent of Mercy. She still rises early.

Quietly, an old-world gentility almost conce-

At a time when the country did not have one ballet school, it was an impossible dream. Taking her considerable courage in both hands, she opened a studio in Patrick Street

The Firkin Crane building at the old Cork Butter Market, now being restored as the home of the Ballet.

—and made it come true

Below: Paul McCarthy.

Paul McCarthy began his career in the arts in his native Cork, before receiving training and experience in business and finance in the UK. In the early 1990's he returned home. Paul has worked with the Royal Shakespeare Company and Riverdance, and for the Belfast Festival at Queens, the Dublin Theatre Festival and the Edinburgh Fringe. Locally, Paul has production-managed many major festivals in Cork city. In 2006 he became director of the Firkin Crane. He has concentrated on developing it as a centre of excellence for dance with a strong local, national and international remit. With Paul at the helm, the dance activity in this unique building has increased fivefold and is recognised by the Arts Council as a vital resource for dance in Ireland.

Joan Denise Moriarty School of Dance

—— Est. 1945 ——

Celebrating 55 Years

The Joan Denise Moriarty School of Dance

The Joan Denise Moriarty School of Dance was founded in 1940. It was the 'mother' of many Moriarty schools established across Munster.

Moriarty bequeathed her School to her student and member of Cork Ballet Company, Breda Quinn, who ran it, together with another Moriarty student, Sinéad Murphy, from 1992 until her death in 2009. The School is now run by Breda's family. The teachers, Maeve Kelleher and Alexandra Archer, were both Moriarty-trained and members of Cork Ballet Company.

Facing page, insert:
The late Breda Quinn, director of the Moriarty School of Dance.

Main image: A flyer celebrating 55 years of the Joan Denise Moriarty School of Dance and below; 2 Nov 1995: Performance to mark the 75th anniversary of the Royal Academy of Dancing at the Moriarty School, Emmet Place, Cork. It was the Academy's first official function in the city. Students attended from all the schools of dancing in the city, and from Dublin and Limerick.
(Courtesy of the *Irish Examiner*)

The Moriarty Legacy: The Dance Schools

The Cork School of Dance

Sinéad Murphy

In 1978 I began a journey that shaped my life. Under the watchful, caring and encouraging eyes of Joan Denise Moriarty I began to train as a dance student in her school at 1B Emmet Place, Cork. In 1987 I felt honoured and privileged when she invited me to train as a teacher with her. For the first five years of my training I had the wonderful experience of Miss Moriarty at my side. Under her guidance I gained my teaching qualifications in 1992, the year of her death. Inspired by her I continued to further my career and gained Fellowship status of the Imperial Society of Teachers of Dancing and I am now an international ballet examiner. I taught in Miss Moriarty's school until 2009, when I opened my own school, Cork School of Dance, in the Firkin Crane, a building that was very close to her heart. Following her example, I encourage my students to take exams, I give them the opportunity to perform in public regularly, and choreograph new ballets specially for them.

On my first day of teaching with her, Miss Moriarty gave me a gift of an ornamental owl with a handwritten note saying: 'This little owl will always watch over you.' I still treasure it. Miss Moriarty, I believe that it is

your wise spirit which is watching over me and all my students. They never met you but I feel they know you, your beliefs and your unending love of dance, through me. Without you, your tireless dedication, your boundless energy and your 'never say can't' attitude, we would not have the rich dance heritage that we have today in Ireland and especially here in Cork.

Miss Moriarty had a huge impact on my professional life, as on that of so many others, and she taught me so much, not just about dance but also about integrity and determination. She has left us an inspiring legacy of dance, a vision, and a discipline that many say is lost in the society of today. I like to think that in some small way I am passing on Miss Moriarty's legacy to my own students.

Sinéad Murphy, F.I.S.T.D. Examiner, RADTC, A.L.C.M. is Director of the Cork School of Dance at the Firkin Crane Dance Centre. She is an international ballet examiner and choreographer with over 20 years of teaching experience, having been a student of Joan Denise Moriarty, the leading lady in establishing the Firkin Crane as the home of dance in Cork.

Cork City Ballet

Alan Foley

'Attitude is a choice. The most important one you'll ever make.'

Viktor Frankl

Joan Denise Moriarty demonstrated this with her work for ballet in Ireland, displaying extraordinary tenacity and even audacity in her endeavours to achieve recognition for this art form, which was relatively unknown in most parts of the isolated and puritanical Ireland of the mid-twentieth century.

I was fourteen years old when I first encountered this formidable woman and she frightened the life out of me. 'To become a dancer you have to study art, music, drama and sculpture', she proclaimed. I remember this so well because its truth gradually became evident to me, especially once I had founded my own company, had become a choreographer, and discovered how many of the arts are involved in a good ballet production.

I fled after my initial encounter with JDM but returned the following year to study in her school and dance with the Cork Ballet Company for many years. It was here under her guidance that my love of classical ballet was nurtured whilst encountering some of the world's greatest dancers in her large-scale productions, including the Hungarian ballet star Zoltan Solymosi, who went on to partner Darcey Bussell and Sylvie Guillem at London's Royal Ballet.

Subsequent training in Russia, New York and London rewarded me with a Fellowship in the teaching of classical ballet from the Imperial Society of Teachers of Dancing in 1998.

Cork City Ballet was formed in 1991, and had its first performance at the Everyman Palace Theatre in Cork in March, 1992. Now in receipt of regular Arts Council and Cork City Council funding, we have forged fruitful partnerships with organisations including the Cork Opera House and the Firkin Crane – the historic building originally acquired by JDM as a home for Irish National Ballet.

As JDM did, we present the great classical ballets to the people of

Left:
Poster for the Irish tour of Cork City Ballet's *Ballet Spectacular 2006* featuring *La Bayadère* 2006, with International Stars Dragos Mihalcea and Marie Lindqvist

Right: Cork City Ballet, *Swan Lake* 2010 at Cork Opera House

Page 66, Cork City Ballet, *Giselle* 2011

Cork. Like her, we include contemporary dance in our repertoire and new works specially choreographed for our company. Like her, we bring our shows to as many centres in Ireland as possible.

We are involved in dance in education with our Dance Diploma courses at the College of Further Education, Coláiste Stiofáin Naofa, and with our schools in Firkin Crane.

We collaborate with dance organisations in Ireland, in particular Irish National Youth Ballet and Irish Russian Youth Ballet, and have established close links with ballet companies abroad, both in Russia and the UK.

The setting up of a full-time professional ballet company remains an objective. I feel proud that our work carried out in the tradition and spirit of JDM is helping to create the conditions for this to happen. The magnificent achievement of this remarkable woman from Cork continues to inspire us in this endeavour.

From top, left to right: Alan Foley in *Le Corsaire*, Fennelle Cook, Kevin Hayes, *Giselle* 2011 with Akzhol Mussakhanov, Patricia Crosbie and Monica Loughman, Cork City Ballet principal dancers, Janet Dillon administrator, Alan Foley at the launch of *Ballet through the Lens* with Mary Clarke, editor of *The Dancing Times*, Cork 2006

Alan Foley, founder and artistic director of Cork City Ballet, trained with Joan Denise Moriarty from the age of 15. He continued his studies at the Vaganova (Kirov) Ballet Summer School in Russia in 1989, thereafter in New York and in London. In 1998 he was awarded the Fellowship Diploma in Classical Ballet of the Imperial Society of Teachers of Dancing in London. He has choreographed and produced all Cork City Ballet's productions since 1992, bringing dancers to Cork from the Kirov Ballet, Perm State Ballet of Russia, Royal Swedish Ballet; he has toured to all the major venues in Ireland. He is principal of the Alan Foley Academy of Dance, and director of the VEC Diploma in Dance course at Coláiste Stiofáin Naofa, based at the Firkin Crane in Cork.

Joan Denise Moriarty Commemorated

Clockwise from top left: Firkin Crane exhibition curators Monica Gavin and Breda Quinn, 1997.

Joan Denise Moriarty Founder of Irish National Ballet book published by Mercier Press, 1998. Moriarty Exhibition, 2009.

Cork City Library, Exhibition marking the 60th anniversary of the founding of the Cork Ballet Company by Joan Denise Moriarty, Dec 11, 2007; at the opening: the curators of the exhibition and members of CBC Cherry O'Keefe, Breda Quinn, Monica Gavin with the Deputy Lord Mayor of Cork, Cllr Terry Shannon

Cork City Ballet

Artistic Director: Alan Foley
(in association with Cork Opera House)

presents

GISELLE

Cork Opera House
Thurs 17th - Sat 19th Nov
www.corkoperahouse.ie

Wexford Opera House
Monday 21st Nov
www.wexfordoperahouse.ie

CORK CITY BALLET
Artistic Director: Alan Foley
in association with the Firkin Crane

presents

Aloys Fleischmann
Music for
the Ballet

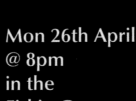

Mon 26th April
@ 8pm
in the
Firkin Crane

Tickets €20
Booking 021-4507487

CORK CITY Ballet
Artistic Director: Alan Foley
in association with Firkin Crane
presents

JOAN DENISE
MORIARTY

CENTENARY 2012

Centenary Gala

Clockwise from top left
Moriarty exhibition
Bishopstown, former
CBC dancers, 2009.

Cork City Library talk

Cork City Ballet,
Firkin Crane,
Moriarty Gala 2012

2010 Fleischmann Cen
Moriarty exhibition an

Cork City Ballet *Gisell*
November 2011

Further Reading

Seán O'Faoláin, *She Had To Do Something* (London, Jonathan Cape, 1938) – a comedy on the turmoil caused by the visit of a foreign ballet company to 'a small provincial city on the seaboard'

Michael MacLiammóir, Michael Bowles, Cepta Cullen: 'Design for a Ballet', *The Bell*, Vol. 4, No. 6 (Dublin, Sept. 1942)

Joseph Reade: 'Irish Ballet', *The Bell*, Vol. 6, No. 1 (Dublin, April 1943)

Aloys Fleischmann (Ed.), *Music in Ireland: A Symposium* (Cork, 1952)

Joseph Gilmore, 'The Cork Ballet Company', Threshold, Vol 1, No. 3, 1957

Ninette de Valois: *Come Dance with Me – A Memoir 1898-1956* (London, 1957; Dublin, 1992)

Norris Davidson: 'Ballet in Ireland', *Dance and Dancers* (Dublin, Jan. 1961)

Fay Werner: 'Ballet in Ireland', *Dancing Times* (London, June 1964) 470-2

Marie Rambert: *Quicksilver – The Autobiography of Marie Rambert* (London, 1972)

Ciarán Benson: *The Place of the Arts in Irish Education* (Dublin, 1979)

Carolyn Swift: 'Dance in Ireland', *Bulletin of the Department of Foreign Affairs*, No. 996 (Dublin, March 1983) 2-6

Peter Brinson: *The Dancer and the Dance: Developing Theatre Dance in Ireland* (Dublin, 1985)

Brian P. Kennedy: *Dreams and Responsibilities: The State and the Arts in Independent Ireland* (Dublin, Arts Council of Ireland, n.d. [1988])

Carolyn Swift: 'End of an Era: Joan Moriarty', *Dance News Ireland*, Spring 1992, 12

Ruth Fleischmann (Ed.): *Joan Denise Moriarty: Founder of Irish National Ballet – Material for a History of Dance in Ireland* (Cork, 1998)

Anna Leatherdale and Victoria Todd: *Shall we dance? A Report on Vocational Dance Training in Ireland* (Dublin, 1998)

Ruth Fleischmann (Ed.): *Aloys Fleischmann (1910-1992) A Life for Music in Ireland Remembered by Contemporaries* (Cork, 2000)

Tomás Ó Canainn: *Seán Ó Riada – His Life and Work* (Cork, 2003)

Diana Theodores (Ed.): *Dancing on the Edge of Europe: Irish Choreographers in Conversation* (Cork, 2003)

Monica Loughman with Jean Harrington: *The Irish Ballerina* (Dublin, 2004)

Alicia St. Leger: *Melodies and Memories: 150 Years at Cork Opera House* (Cork, 2005)

Séamas de Barra: *Aloys Fleischmann* (Dublin, 2006)

Foley and Loughmann: *A Portrait - Ballet through the Lens*, with a Foreword by Mary Clarke (Cork, 2006)

Deirdre Mulrooney): *Irish Moves - An Illustrated History of Dance and Physical Theatre in Ireland* with a Foreword by Declan Kiberd (Dublin, 2006)

Arts Council of Ireland: *Towards a strategy of support for Professional Ballet in Ireland:* Summary Draft Report based on research by Derek Purnell in 2006 (Dublin, 2007)

Anne Bernadette Quill, *The Elite and the Oppressed: The Rise and Fall of Irish National Ballet*, Master of Arts (Dance) thesis (University of Limerick, July 2007)

Alan Foley, *Cork City Ballet: The Story So Far*, Cork 2008

Patrick Zuk: *A J. Potter (1918-1980): The career and creative achievement of an Irish composer in social and cultural context* (PhD, Durham University UK, 2008)

Mary Clarke: 'Music for the Ballet', *Dancing Times*, April 2010

Benjamin Dwyer, *Constellations: The Life and Music of John Buckley* (Dublin, 2011)

Victoria O'Brien: *A History of Irish Ballet from 1927 to 1963* (Oxford, 2011)

Patricia Crosbie: *Reaching through the Mirror: An Autoethnography of an Irish Ballet Dancer*, Master of Arts (Dance) thesis (University of Limerick, Sep. 2011)

Mary Clarke: 'First Lady of Irish Ballet', *Dancing Times*, Oct 2011

Joan Denise Moriarty 1912(?)-1992

No documentation of Moriarty's life before 1930 has come to light

?-1933	Resident in Liverpool with her mother, a native of Mallow
1931	Wins the Irish Step Dance Championship of England
1932	Highly commended for solo war pipes in the Tailtean Games, Croke Park, Dublin
1933	Wins the Munster Open Championship for solo war pipes
1933 Sept.	The Moriarty family returns to Mallow
1934	Moriarty begins to teach dance there and, from 1938, weekly in Cork
1940 Feb.	Death of Moriarty's mother, Marion Moriarty
1940 Nov.	Moriarty School of Dance set up in Cork
1947	First performance, in the Cork Opera House, of the Cork Ballet Group, later re-named Cork Ballet Company, with the Cork Symphony Orchestra
1948-93	Annual Cork Ballet Week
1956-93	Guest producers and dancers in the annual Cork Ballet Company performances
1950-70	Moriarty attends Royal Academy and other ballet summer schools in England
1959	Founding of Ireland's first professional ballet company, Irish Theatre Ballet
1959-64	Irish Theatre Ballet performs all over Ireland, north and south
1963-64	Irish Theatre Ballet merged with Patricia Ryan's Dublin National Ballet
1964	Closure of the merged company: Irish National Ballet
1970-73	Cork Ballet Company performs in Dublin's Abbey and Gaiety Theatres
1973	Founding of the second professional company, Irish Ballet Company, later re-named Irish National Ballet
1973-89	The professional company travels the country during two annual touring seasons
1978-84	Moriarty's *Playboy of the Western World* travels to Dublin, Belfast, New York, London and Rennes
1979	Honorary Doctorate of the National University of Ireland
1984	The Arts Council of Ireland commissions a report on dance from Peter Brinson
1985	Publication of the report; Moriarty resigns from Irish National Ballet
1988	Arts Council withdrawal of funding to Irish National Ballet
1989	Closure of Irish National Ballet
1992 Jan 24	Death of Joan Denise Moriarty
1993	Final performance of Cork Ballet Company

Acknowledgements

Archival research: Kitty Buckley, Anne Fleischmann, Monica Gavin

Digital photography: Max Fleischmann

My thanks to:

Liam Ronayne, Cork City Librarian, and to Kitty Buckley, Executive Librarian Music Library, for granting access to the Moriarty Collection and for invaluable assistance

Catriona Mulcahy, Archivist, University College Cork, for her kindness in facilitating the family's work on the Fleischmann Collection

Cork City & County Archives for access to the Patrick Murray Collection

RTÉ Stills Archive for permission to reproduce two images from *Lugh of the Golden Arm* © RTÉ Stills Library

The Evening Echo, The Irish Examiner, The Irish Times for permission to reproduce Moriarty material

Lavinia Anderson, the late Hilda Buckley, Julia Cotter, Patricia Crosbie, Anne and Pat Fleming, Monica Gavin, Enid Lass, Cherry O'Keefe for granting us access to their private Cork Ballet Company, CBC Folk Dance Group, Irish Theatre Ballet and Irish Ballet Company / Irish National Ballet photograph and programme collections; to all of these and Joanna Banks, Jill d'Alton, Anna Donovan, Domy Reiter-Soffer for patient help in identifying performances and dancers

John Buckley for providing images of his ballet *Diúltú*

Alan Foley for permission to reproduce images from his 2011 Cork City Ballet *Giselle* programme

Angela Goff for creating images of orchestral and piano score pages

Tomás Ó Canainn for permission to reproduce the Ó Riada image on the cover of his Ó Riada book

Gerard O'Meara of Mallow for permission to reproduce his Irish National Ballet photograph

Peadar Ó Riada for permission to reproduce a Seán Ó Riada letter

Provision and RD Photo for permission to reproduce the Cork School of Dance images

Cover photograph: Joan Denise Moriarty by James McAnally